HISTORY OF PETS
THE HISTORY OF PET BIRDS

by Alicia Z. Klepeis

pogo

Ideas for Parents and Teachers

Pogo Books let children practice reading informational text while introducing them to nonfiction features such as headings, labels, sidebars, maps, and diagrams, as well as a table of contents, glossary, and index.

Carefully leveled text with a strong photo match offers early fluent readers the support they need to succeed.

Before Reading

- "Walk" through the book and point out the various nonfiction features. Ask the student what purpose each feature serves.
- Look at the glossary together. Read and discuss the words.

Read the Book

- Have the child read the book independently.
- Invite him or her to list questions that arise from reading.

After Reading

- Discuss the child's questions. Talk about how he or she might find answers to those questions.
- Prompt the child to think more. Ask: Do you have a pet bird or know someone who does? Do you think birds make good pets? Why or why not?

Pogo Books are published by Jump!
5357 Penn Avenue South
Minneapolis, MN 55419
www.jumplibrary.com

Library of Congress Cataloging-in-Publication Data

Names: Klepeis, Alicia, 1971– author.
Title: The history of pet birds / by Alicia Z. Klepeis.
Description: Minneapolis, MN: Jump!, Inc., [2024]
Series: History of pets | Includes index.
Audience: Ages 7-10
Identifiers: LCCN 2022061239 (print)
LCCN 2022061240 (ebook)
ISBN 9798885246040 (hardcover)
ISBN 9798885246057 (paperback)
ISBN 9798885246064 (ebook)
Subjects: LCSH: Cage birds—Juvenile literature.
Cage birds—History—Juvenile literature.
Classification: LCC SF461.35 .K54 2024 (print)
LCC SF461.35 (ebook)
DDC 636.6/8—dc23/eng/20230215
LC record available at https://lccn.loc.gov/2022061239
LC ebook record available at https://lccn.loc.gov/2022061240

Editor: Eliza Leahy
Designer: Emma Almgren-Bersie

Photo Credits: Eric Isselee/Shutterstock, cover, 1, 22br; xpixel/Shutterstock, 3; Vitaly Titov/Shutterstock, 4; Stephen Denness/Dreamstime, 5; Cultural Archive/Alamy, 6; duncan1890/iStock, 7; Gado Images/Alamy, 8-9; Artokoloro/Alamy, 10-11; Classic Image/Alamy, 12-13; UrosPoteko/iStock, 14-15; Christine_Kohler/iStock, 16; aluxum/iStock, 17; Catatan Bunda/Shutterstock, 18-19 (foreground); qoppi/Shutterstock, 18-19 (background); Elena..D/Shutterstock, 20-21; Feng Yu/Shutterstock, 22tl; cynoclub/Shutterstock, 22tr, 23; photomaster/Shutterstock, 22ml; Tracy Starr/Shutterstock, 22mr; Avramchuk Igor/Shutterstock, 22bl.

Printed in the United States of America at Corporate Graphics in North Mankato, Minnesota.

TABLE OF CONTENTS

CHAPTER 1

FEATHERED FRIENDS

A pet parakeet flies around its owner's home. It lands on its owner's finger.

 parakeet ·····▶

The pet bird and its owner **bond**. Birds were once only wild. When did people start keeping them as pets? Let's find out!

CHAPTER 2

AROUND THE GLOBE

People have kept pet birds for thousands of years. How do we know? **Ancient** Greek artists showed pet birds in sculptures. Ancient Romans wrote poems and stories about them.

ancient sculpture ....▶

parrot

During that time, most people kept **native** birds as pets. Ancient Greeks and Romans had pet doves, ducks, and geese. Ancient South Americans, Asians, and Africans had pet parrots.

In China, pigeons have been pets for more than 1,000 years. Why? Pigeons are calm. They are also smart. They can even be **trained** to carry messages!

As people traveled the globe, they trapped **exotic** birds. Troops from **Macedonia** reached India in 327 BCE. Some took parrots back to Europe.

Royalty and wealthy people kept parrots as pets. Why? These birds were rare. They were expensive to buy.

DID YOU KNOW?

Some owners kept their parrots in cages made of silver!

From the 1400s to the 1600s, people from European countries started exploring the world. Traders and explorers moved birds from one area to another. Exotic pet birds became more common.

People took many **tropical** birds to colder areas. Christopher Columbus brought an Amazon parrot to Europe. **Merchants** from Italy brought home canaries from islands off the African coast.

Starlings are native to Europe. They were popular pets in the 1600s. People taught the birds to **pipe**. Some people taught them to talk! How? They repeated words to help the birds learn. People still do this today.

WHAT DO YOU THINK?

Foresters in Germany took bullfinch **chicks** from their nests. They raised the birds. They played songs on flutes. The chicks **mimicked** the songs. Do you think animals should be taken from the wild? Why or why not?

starling

CHAPTER 3

PETS FOR ALL PEOPLE

Over time, birds became available to most people. The canary is one example. In the 1500s, they were too expensive for most people to own. But by the mid-1800s, everyday people owned them.

canary

Canaries are still popular pets. Why? They sing beautifully. They play with toys. They are good company.

Birds that can talk, like budgies or cockatoos, are popular, too. Many parrots and parakeets can also talk.

Parrots and other birds have worked as **therapy** animals. Why? Their singing calms people. Talking birds can say calming things.

TAKE A LOOK!

In which states are birds the most popular pets after cats and dogs? Take a look!

- ■ Florida
- ■ Iowa
- ■ Louisiana
- ■ Massachusetts
- ■ North Dakota
- ■ Ohio
- ■ Oklahoma

Many owners hold their birds. We know this is good for the bird's brain. It makes the owner happy, too. Would you like a pet bird?

WHAT DO YOU THINK?

Some people play music for their feathered friends. What kind of music would you play for your pet bird? Why?

QUICK FACTS & TOOLS

MOST POPULAR U.S. PET BIRD BREEDS

1. parakeet

2. cockatiel

3. canary

4. conure

5. African gray parrot

6. Amazon parrot

ancient: Belonging to a period long ago.

bond: To form a close relationship with someone, such as a pet or family member.

chicks: Baby birds.

exotic: From a faraway country.

foresters: People who plant and take care of trees or forests.

Macedonia: An ancient European kingdom located north of Greece.

merchants: People who buy and sell items to make money.

mimicked: Imitated or copied closely.

native: An animal or plant that lives or grows naturally in a certain place.

perch: A bar or branch on which a bird can rest.

pipe: To make a high-pitched sound.

royalty: Members of a royal family, such as kings or queens.

therapy: Relating to treatment of mental or physical disorders.

trained: Taught to perform a skill.

tropical: Of or having to do with the hot, rainy area of the tropics.

INDEX

TO LEARN MORE

Finding more information is as easy as 1, 2, 3.

❶ Go to www.factsurfer.com

❷ Enter "thehistoryofpetbirds" into the search box.

❸ Choose your book to see a list of websites.

FACT SURFER